White Goat Black Sheep

poems by

Kimberly Ann Priest

Finishing Line Press
Georgetown, Kentucky

White Goat Black Sheep

Copyright © 2017 by Kimberly Ann Priest
ISBN 978-1-63534-379-3 First Edition
All rights reserved under International and Pan-American Copyright Conventions. No part of this book may be reproduced in any manner whatsoever without written permission from the publisher, except in the case of brief quotations embodied in critical articles and reviews.

ACKNOWLEDGMENTS

Special thanks to poet Paige Ackerson-Kiely for her expert guidance and dedicated attention to my work.

Publisher: Leah Maines

Editor: Christen Kincaid

Cover Art: Kathleen Mekailek

Author Photo: Heather Horner

Cover Design: Elizabeth Maines McCleavy

Printed in the USA on acid-free paper.
Order online: www.finishinglinepress.com
also available on amazon.com

Author inquiries and mail orders:
Finishing Line Press
P. O. Box 1626
Georgetown, Kentucky 40324
U. S. A.

Table of Contents

I.	page 1
II.	page 2
III.	page 3
IV.	page 4
V.	page 5
VI.	page 6
VII.	page 7
VIII.	page 8
IX.	page 9
X.	page 10
XI.	page 11
XII.	page 12
XIII.	page 13
XIV.	page 14
XV.	page 15
XVI.	page 16
XVII.	page 17
XVIII.	page 18
XIX.	page 19
XX.	page 20
XXI.	page 21
XXII.	page 22
XXIII.	page 23
XXIV.	page 24

for Jenny

I.

Your tiny hand telling me
to tie us up with ribbon, bind us,

bring a piece of tree to the ceremony and see how it
won't grow.

One of your smiles is hanging from a rope.
Both of the children are looking for their mother:

me,

and you little sister,
smearing mud across a canvas I have painted:

perfectly white rows of perfectly round trees.

II.

When I saw your unformed body, pink, I turned away;
you were bloody and had two perfect feet.

I told mother I did not want to see you, a sister.

I did not want to see your puckered face.

I did not want to hold it like ripe fruit, bite,
feel your muscle kicking in my teeth.

You were closer to me than breath

as if I were the finger dividing your infant legs from their sleeves,
drawing furrows into your most unknowing place.

Rocks and pebbles.
Your body going to seed.

I would bury you
but am fearful the mound might resemble a tomb.

III.

The curators are realigning trees, inspecting bark,
naming,

not telling the truth:

> Like men walking they are.
> Like roots watching.
> Like ears learning first to touch
>   then smell and see.

My little sister who will not wear the shiny white shoes.

I try to put them on her.
I try to tie them to her feet.
I try to be patient, drink the silence,

but it keeps fondling me.

IV.

I think I am the part of a man he wants to forget.
I think I am a bone.

Little sister, I think we are two disjointed lines
stretched across a page:
You and I.

Little sister, I think we are in rows and there is
breath between us.

I think it is a long breath with
water above, water beneath.

I think of an expanse, how it stretches across a horizon,
how your eyes are like its fire:

deep, deep, deep, and calling to me.

V.

Black goat. White goat. Black goat. White goat.

This is the ceremony of the parting of the goats.

You wear Goth, little sister,
braiding your hair, dividing your scalp,
huddled near the bathrooms at school laden with graffiti:
Jess + Jonny, Ally + Blain.

I wear my hair in long, long streams.
I sit by the river, gather moss, varnish weeds.

I will contain us, build an altar, bind it with
my feet.

Little sister,
make a bed out of some hay. Lie down, lie down,

little sheep.

VI.

This is the dance of the reeds,
the arousal of persimmons.

The river has flooded and frightened all the sheep.

But the trees don't lean.

> *Don't lean, little sister!*
> *Don't bend like a reed.*

Don't bend: our bruise, my break,

cut off like a branch in the river,
a pen stroke my hand can't repeat.

Lines so difficult
they bleed.

VII.

The hours stretch against his body:
the part of a man I want to forget.

Strong crow,
       over-limbed,
             dark leaf, dark leaf.

You grow yourself into trees.

Oh to be like the river.
Oh to move like a sleep.
Oh to be fluid and holding my breath—

your long bony fingers too feathered to live
in my deep.

VIII.

I pluck a string: you did not hear it.
I strum a tune: you turn away.

> White goat.
> Black sheep.

Neither you or I, little sister, know this masquerade.

But we will learn,
one river bend at a time.
One bruise, one break.

You move toward the men with pruning sheers and cables.

I search for string to bind you, fill your mouth with choices:
a variety of seeds.

IX.

The curators are painting the trees with white dots:
a modest graffiti.

I point to the tree in the river and say it is not like the others:
see how it wades knee deep but does not sway?

No one responds to this.

I wade into the water and touch the skin of the tree inspirited
with aphids, yet it does not die.

I ask the skin how it thrives.
I ask the skin to speak to me.

It does not answer; I peel back my own bark to see it is
inspirited too.

X.

I have a little sister and she is not yet grown.

I offer her persimmons.
She says they taste like stones.

I offer her a paintbrush.
She says it feels like paint.

I watch her try to form a row of sheep across a page.

But she is like the page and cannot know the rows she makes.

I offer her some honey.
and she eats it down, down, slow,

she says it tickles in her tummy, calling her by name.

XI.

Our mother gathers cloth by the river,
opens a box and pulls out some thread.

She sews my sister to a rock.

I watch my sister strain.

Our mother wades into the river,
brings us each a pebble from its bed,
tells us to hold it in our cheeks.

We hold the pebbles.

Swallow, she says.

The stone falls hard into my belly:
I am filled.

I see my feet are naked, with a separation in between.

XII.

I take back the ripe persimmons I gave to my sister.
Black sheep. Black sheep.

She has filled a bowl with their seeds.
Now one of her smiles floats among the shells.
She reaches to peel it away.

We fight over the smile, a ribbon between us. *Bleat. Bleat.*

We will not be bound to anything!
Black goat. White sheep.

XIII.

I want to peel back your bark and show you the aphids
to see if they are like mine.
But you are always moving, little sister,
and telling me to move.

There are long white scratches on your arms.

I think you are scratching because of the aphids.

I do not scratch; I am older than you and know
the curators will see it.

I choose a smooth stone from the riverbed, rubbing it slowly
over each wound. It feels like polishing a whisper

and murmurs into a dying spring.

XIV.

The curators have siphoned bruised wine from a tree.

They drink.

They drink until drunk on its honey

and lull in the shade of the tree examining
white dots from a distance
while tarnishing the river with spit.

I spit.

Suzy & Sally have hearted their names on your arm,
little sister.

You bleed.

I search for mother's thread box to stitch up the places
you bleed.

XV.

There are fresh pools of paint near the cattails by the river.

You have found your feet, little sister!
You light up like a wall of graffiti, artwork needled over
your stomach, thighs, and cheeks.

You are a yowling bathroom stall.
I cannot cover you enough.

My small body.

Your small body.

Our mother scrubbing with pebbles by the river.
Our mother going to seed.
Our mother with needle and thread by the river.

Our mother, our mother— the altar too distant to reach.

XVI.

There are hundreds of little sisters by the river.

They wear smocks.
They fatten and feed.

They show their bellies to trees by the river,
snarling, laughing, rolling their feet.

My sister is nearing the river!

searching smocks, reaching moss,
lifting bark haunted with crows;

forgetting stone and seed, *forgetting river,*
forgetting its current and clay-bottomed hand.

I am watching the tree in the river.

Little sister,
if it tries to curse you, I'll lift my bark,
show it the row of teeth marks ribbing over me.

XVII.

I and the river are tarnished.
See how we linger with blood.

Notice the rust in our waters, crushed like a fire at dawn
roaming the hills of an altar, roaming the body it takes.

All of my lines are a carcass. All of my bones altercate.

XVIII.

Death like a blanket:
how warm you are on your alter of sleep,
little sister,

black sheep.

Soft like a crow under shadow
dark and seasoned by rain;

one of your whispers is slipping my grasp.

I flute you a river of choices.
I sing you a mercy mossing with grief.

Don't cry for white dots on a canvas;
don't poke at the carvings beneath.

Don't reel at the sight of a fresh mound of dirt entangling the roots
where the aphids now feed.

It's not you buried there little sister.
No, it's not you little sheep.

XIX.

Furrows thread the earth as mother unbraids
her box of long streams.

Bleat bleat, you cry, *bleat bleat.*

I cover my sides stitched with aphids;
I cover the wounds where they bite and I bleed.

But you, little sister, writhing with honey,
sticky with streaks run down your legs—

you wake in a dream of dark shadows rejoicing,
you wake in the shape of their wings.

The roots of your tongue have been searching

the mouths of other black sheep.

XX.

The curators whitewash the bathroom;
our mother washes your legs.

I wash off all the whispers stirring in our bed.

Little sister,
        we have shared too much.

Too much of the bend of the river,
too much of the limbs that quiver and quake,
too much in the eye of a dark crow at night,
too much in the absence of knowledge,

too much of this tree that we eat from
for good and evil's sake.

XXI.

Sadist in the shadow
lifting your umber belly of bark in the hallway near the bathroom
where the unthreaded go to pray,

> *I am old enough to know.*

How many fingers will you count into my sister as she dreams?

How many dark shadows will you summon from her thighs?

How many times will my mother dry the pee from her ankles,
impatient with pleas for a good night's sleep?

How many puddles of my sister will seep under my feet?

How will I ask her forgiveness someday when we are older
for the mornings I hated this altar

and the sheepish form her body now takes?

XXII.

At the tree where knowledge grows,

I hand you a pocket of seed, little sister:
round stones that cling to its roots.

Eat, I say like our mother,
eat.

And we do.

They are smooth and red like the river,
they are filling our bellies like food;

> clean stones, smooth stone,
>
> red stones, red stones,
>
> red mouth:
>
> three stones, three stones: three seeds,
>
> three seeds grow roots, those roots grow deep,
>
> those roots to keep,
>
> our souls will bleat:
>
> *white goat, black sheep eat eat.*
>
> *hold us in place when anyone binds up our feet.*

XXIII.

The waters above are not the waters beneath.

This, the curators don't tell us but, this
we already know.

Black goat, black goat, white goat, white sheep,
spotted, speckled, plain,
Janice & Jonny + Ira or Pete:

      too many separations.

Bleat bleat little sister, *bleat bleat.* Your bruise,
my break.

The waters above are still searching
the waters above will make rain.

XXIV.

I have a little sister and she is nearly grown.

I offer her my secret,
she crows and scrapes her teeth.

I have a little sister whose sides, unstitched,
still bleed.

I have a little sister keeping secrets from me.

Lie down, little sister, your death no more than a sleep.

Lie down, little sister, sweet suffering little dark sheep.

Kimberly Ann Priest is an MFA graduate in Creative Writing from New England College, already holding an MA in English Language & Literature from Central Michigan University. A proud Michigan native, she has taught composition and creative writing courses for Central Michigan University and Alma College, and participated in local initiatives to increase awareness concerning sexual assault and domestic violence issues. Her academic and creative writing carefully observes the intersections between motherhood, violence, religion, sexual identity, and trauma, teasing story out of vulnerability and shame.

Kimberly's poetry has appeared in several literary journals including *The 3288 Review, Temenos, Borderlands: The Texas Poetry Review, The West Texas Literary Review, Windhover, Ruminate Magazine* and *The Berkeley Poetry Review* and she has been nominated for two Pushcart Prizes. Currently, she is an Instructor of English at Oklahoma Baptist University and an editor for the *Nimrod International Journal of Prose and Poetry*.

www.ingramcontent.com/pod-product-compliance
Lightning Source LLC
LaVergne TN
LVHW040118080426
835507LV00041B/1723